TED Books

Broken Places & Outer Spaces

Finding Creativity in the Unexpected

NNEDI OKORAFOR

ILLUSTRATIONS BY SHYAMA GOLDEN

Simon & Schuster

New York London Toronto Sydney New Delhi

Simon & Schuster
1230 Avenue of the Americas
New York, NY 10020

First Simon & Schuster hardcover edition June 2019
SIMON & SCHUSTER and colophon are registered trademarks of Simon & Schuster, Inc.

For information about special discounts for bulk purchases, please contact Simon & Schuster Special Sales at 1-866-506-1949 or business@simonandschuster.com.

The Simon & Schuster Speakers Bureau can bring authors to your live event. For more information or to book an event contact the Simon & Schuster Speakers Bureau at 1-866-248-3049 or visit our website at www.simonspeakers.com.

Interior design by MGMT. design
Jacket design by MGMT. design
Illustrations by Shyama Golden

Manufactured in the United States of America

10 9 8 7 6 5 4 3 2 1

Library of Congress Cataloging-in-Publication Data is available.

ISBN 978-1-5011-9547-1
ISBN 978-1-5011-9548-8 (ebook)

I dedicate this book to my mother Dr. Helen Okorafor,
the most powerful woman I've ever known.

CONTENTS

Broken Places & Outer Spaces

When the caterpillar in its chrysalis is changing into a butterfly, does it think it's dying?

—Oubria Tronshaw, writer

When I was lying there in the VA hospital with a big hole blown through the middle of my life, I started having these dreams of flying. I was free.

—Jake Sully, from *Avatar*

1 Beached

The beach was just the way I loved it: empty, its waters comfortable and clear, a few sand crabs dashing around. The air was warm, it was sunny, and the strong wind danced wildly. I had all the time in the world. I stood facing the water, strong but always somewhat unsteady. I had to concentrate more than most on the strength and direction of the wind, focusing my eyes ahead so that I wouldn't embarrass myself by stumbling. Since the incident two decades ago, I'd been this way.

My toes had to work hard to grasp and feel the sand. The undersides of my feet tingled softly, as if I were eternally walking on a bed of AstroTurf. The area from my ankles to my knees always felt not quite there, vague and elemental. My thighs were strong, the most vibrant part of my legs. My strange curved back was forever pushing me a bit forward. It had been so many years, one would think by now I'd be accustomed to my body feeling this way. But my awareness that I'd once been something else had become an essential part of me—a state of being.

In old age, I won't be bent over, thanks to my fused spine and the steel rod lashed to it. I can't wear high heels because of my poor balance. I avoid crowds because standing among many people is like standing in the ocean when the water is whirling around me; I lose my sense of place. When I step onstage in front of large audiences, adrenaline blends with my poor proprioception and this robs me of my balance. The same phenomenon causes me to lose track of my legs while standing.

The wind blew against my back and I stumbled forward. Toward the water. Still, I didn't go in.

There's a strange feeling that I experience before I can go into the ocean. It happens at the point just before the ability to walk stops mattering and the ability to swim begins to matter. This is especially true when it's windy, motion not only in the water, but also in the air. The hypnotic ripples on the surface of the water, the swirling of the air, and the sinking and suction of the sand beneath my feet take my balance away. Before I can get to the point where I am swimming, I have to fall.

I stood there in the nourishing sunshine, thinking about my legs and science fiction. I had recently written about a superheroine for Marvel, a wheelchair-bound girl in Nigeria named Ngozi. She physically and mentally bonds with an alien symbiotic organism named Venom and is thus able to stand up and kick ass. Ngozi made me consider my own proprioceptively challenged body, how it could be augmented with technology and allow me to move about the world with ease and agility. Not as I used to in the first half of my life, but as a cyborg.

My legs would be caged with an exoskeletal machine made of a fine webwork of magnesium alloy. My gait would be so well augmented that I'd be able to leap, run, even cartwheel better than I ever could before it all happened. My spine would be replaced with a strong yet flexible organic substance that would allow me to turn my head all the way around like an owl, support my body, *and* allow me to do epic backbends. With the steel in my back, I already identified as a rudimentary cyborg, part basic machine, so it wouldn't be that much of a leap.

Before the incident, I moved about the world with a sense of ease and entitlement. I was the kid in gym class who everyone always chose first for their team because I was the fastest, could jump the highest, could throw the farthest and hardest, could aim the most accurately. To myself, I was the athlete and the budding scientist. Then quite suddenly everything changed, and I was an athlete drifting in the vacuum of space and I'd lost faith in the sciences.

Before the incident, I was sure I'd be an entomologist. Since I could remember I'd loved and been fascinated by insects, especially those in the orders of Lepidoptera and Orthoptera, butterflies, moths, grasshoppers, and crickets. Praying mantises, too. Creatures with strong legs and unique wings.

In second grade, I built a giant butterfly out of various colors of construction paper. Then I sat on it and waited. And waited. And waited. When the butterfly didn't come to life, happily greet me, and then fly me into the sky, I was depressed for the rest of the day.

I was an imaginative child. Pop-up books were portals to other planets and dimensions, even if they were nonfiction books about human anatomy or the world of birds. I read the Moomin books by Tove Jansson and my imagination exploded even more. As a teen, I consumed horror and fantasy novels as if they were nonfiction. For me, the dark has never been uninhabited. The wind has always brought things. Masquerades are real and the ancestors can be guides.

However, though I'd always loved the sciences, I wasn't born with an interest in science fiction. My journey to writing science fiction did not start with reading it. I didn't discover authors like Octavia Butler and Ursula K. Le Guin until I was already writing about strange planets and advanced societies that use flora-based biotech. And I read Mary Shelley's *Frankenstein* as an annoying book assigned to me in my high school English class.

Growing up, most science fiction novels and films presented boldly white male–dominated worlds where I knew I could never exist on my own terms. In these narratives, I found that I, more often than not, empathized with the aliens/others more than the protagonists, so reading these stories felt more like an attack on my person than an empowerment. I also resisted the themes of exploration with the intent to colonize that ran so strong in these narratives. They never felt right to me (especially being the child of immigrants from an African country colonized by Europeans) or interesting.

Ultimately, I lost my faith in science after an operation left me mysteriously paralyzed from the waist down. It took years, but battling through my paralysis was the very thing that ignited my passion for storytelling and the transformative power of the imagination. And returning to Nigeria brought me back around to the sciences through science fiction, for those family trips to Nigeria were where and why I started wondering and then dreaming about the effects of technology and where it could take us in the future.

This series of openings and awakenings led me to a profound realization: *What we perceive as limitations have the potential to become strengths greater than what we had when we were "normal" or unbroken. In much of science fiction, when something breaks, something greater often emerges from the cracks.* This is a philosophy that positions our toughest experiences not as barriers, but as doorways, and may be the key to us becoming our truest selves.

In Japan there is an art form called kintsugi, which means "golden joinery," to repair something with gold. It treats breaks and repairs as a part of the object's history. In kintsugi, you don't merely fix what's broken, you repair the total object. In doing so, you transform what you have fixed into something more beautiful than it previously was. This is the philosophy that I came to understand was central to my life. Because in order to really live life, you must *live* life. And that is rarely achieved without cracks along the way. There is often a sentiment that we must remain new, unscathed, unscarred, but in order to do this, you must never leave home, never experience, never risk or be harmed, and thus never grow.

As I stood on that beach, I thought, "Yes, a metal alloy exoskeleton around my legs and a spine made of an organic flexible super substance, that would be awesome." I chuckled. "I'd be incredible." Just then, a large wave rolled in and I stumbled forward again. I kissed my teeth with annoyance, turned around, and walked back up the beach. I wasn't ready. But I would get there.

For the moment, I returned to the dry patch of warm sand and lay down. I took a deep cleansing breath and gazed up into the windy sky. I closed my eyes and let the memories tumble forth and roll back until they brought me to the point in time where I became a cyborg.

2 Retrograde

"At this point, Nnedi needs a spinal fusion. Preferably as soon as possible. It's not going to get any better. Her degree of curvature is too advanced." The doctor's voice was full of confidence. He was speaking of surgery, but the tone of his voice said all this was really quite common, standard, textbook, no big deal at all. He looked back and forth between my parents and me, sitting at his desk, his hands teepeed thoughtfully. The doctor was so matter-of-fact, so casual in his delivery that my mind barely registered the severity of what he was saying.

I was halfway into my first year of college, struggling with my chemistry class, enjoying my composition class, detesting my tennis teammates, considering trying out for the university track team, wondering when the next family trip to Nigeria would be and hoping the grunge band Soundgarden came through Chicago in the summer.

"Lots of people have this done, plenty of athletes," he continued. "And they're able to return to their sports some weeks later. Because we're dealing with the spine, there's only a one percent chance of paralysis. Weigh that against imminent respiratory, digestive, and heart problems that will result as the spine compresses the body. If she doesn't have the surgery, by the time Nnedi's twenty-five she'll really be in trouble."

My surgeon was a tall, dark-haired white-bread white man with a kind face and big hands. He was a family man who was good at what he did. If my parents trusted him to do surgery on my spine, I could too. Plus, I was sure everything would be fine. Everything was always fine, especially anything that had to do with my body, which was always together, whole, strong. I refused to let myself see this surgery as a big deal.

Okay.

Fast-forward to the beginning of summer vacation, a few months after deciding to have the surgery. "Change into this," the nurse instructed, handing me a hospital gown. She was a black woman with long red nails and even redder lipstick. The gown was white with almost fluorescent pink stripes on it. *How feminine*, I thought with a humph. I undid my black Doc Martens and set them aside. With a little wiggle my baggy jeans fell easily to the floor. Lastly, I removed my T-shirt with the tree frog on the front and lacy size-34B black bra and folded them all in a neat pile.

Stepping into the hospital gown, I suddenly felt a rush of excitement. In only a few hours I would be corrected. I could get on with my life. Through all the fun of my first year of college, my back problems loomed in the background. Once I'd learned of the surgery date, I'd grow giddy whenever I thought about anything that was to happen after today, May 18. A completely new life.

I imagined rollerblading down the street in a pair of short shorts and a bikini top in the hot sun, not worrying a bit about people staring at my back and how it curved in a weird lopsided *S*. Of course, my parents would chastise me and tell me to put some clothes on and I eventually would, but by choice, not because my back was curved and weird looking and I was self-conscious about this fact.

I walked into the next room in my hospital gown, holding the back closed. The floor was cool and spotless. There were several leather seats lined up against the wall with long gurneys before them. I sat in one of the leather seats. The nurse pursed her red lips, smoothing out her lipstick, and took my pulse and blood pressure. Then she inserted an IV into my vein and told me to count to ten.

"One, two, three . . ."

Fade to black.

• • •

The cause of scoliosis is unknown. Sometimes it is hereditary and other times it is just something else. As if the spine gets this crazy idea to do its own thing without the permission of the rest of the body or the genes in its very cells. Like a restless middle-aged man who leaves his family for a taste of independence. In his frustration and need for freedom, this kind of man always forgets how many people rely on him.

In my case, it was first and foremost science—genetics. I didn't know of any relatives in Nigeria who had scoliosis but my oldest sister, Ifeoma (who is two years my senior), had it, though not as severely as me. When she was younger, she'd had to use an apparatus called a scoliotron at night, which sent electric pulses down the spine. I always wondered what it felt like and one day when I was about ten and she was twelve, I asked Ifeoma to put the gelled pads on my arm and turn it on low.

The first little pulse of electricity felt like spiders crawling underneath the pad, their creepy legs tentatively tapping my skin. Before I knew it, I was running down the hall, jumping down an entire flight of stairs, and fleeing the house. I stood in the middle of the street panting, scratching at my arm until it was reddish brown with irritation.

Ifeoma's scoliosis eventually stabilized on its own. My middle sister, Ngozi (one year my senior), had a mild case, her heavier build working to keep her spine within normal range. And my little brother, Emezie (seven years my junior), who developed scoliosis in his teens, his back eventually stabilized too.

Mine was the scoliosis that wouldn't quit. The irony was that despite (or maybe *because of*) my rabid scoliosis, I had always been a star athlete. It was in my blood. My parents had both been athletes who competed in Nigeria at the collegiate level. My father could leap the hurdles so swiftly that he'd won medals all over the country. My mother could throw the javelin so far that she broke records in Nigeria and won competitions all over Africa. She even made Nigeria's Olympic team in 1964 (the only reason she didn't go was because she'd come down with malaria right before). So it wasn't surprising that my siblings and I grew up to be athletes as well.

From age nine I played semipro tennis. My secret weapons were my killer inside-out forehand and my 114-mile-per-hour serve. But I'd always wanted to try my hand at track and field like my parents. I did so as a senior at Homewood-Flossmoor High School and won twenty-two medals in the 400m, 800m, mile relay, and high jump. Though I did my athletics unhindered, I was diagnosed with scoliosis when I was thirteen.

Despite doing back exercises and wearing a very uncomfortable, oftentimes painful, brace cast from plaster under my clothes for years, my scoliosis worsened. I was like a top-of-the-line robot with a fatal glitch. That's what brought me to this surgery to straighten out and stabilize my spine. As with any surgery involving the spine, there was a risk of paralysis. But choosing between a one percent chance of paralysis and a one hundred percent chance of an early death after a crippled life was a simple decision.

It was May 18, 1993. I was nineteen years old and just back from my first year at the University of Illinois, Urbana-Champaign. I entered the hospital that fateful day on my own two strong legs. I woke up many hours later paralyzed from the waist down. This was the Breaking, and little did I know that it would lead me to become more than I would have ever been without it.

3 Bugs

He was a sweet-looking boy with dark curly hair and stunning blue eyes. He took a deep breath, the smile on his face growing wider. His friends stood behind him in their matching navy blue pants and white shirts, pointing and laughing.

"Nigger daddy longlegs! Nigger daddy longlegs," the boy sang at the top of his lungs. He was laughing so hard he didn't see it coming. I was standing several feet away. Maybe he didn't think my long legs could reach that far. When my foot smashed into his crotch, he yowled and fell to the ground.

"Stupid idiot," I shouted at him, my dark face hot with anger. I hated recess. The only black girl in the fourth grade at Holy Ghost Catholic School, I often felt as if I lived in one of those towns I'd read about in my social studies books. Where dark-skinned people had to walk down the street holding up signs and chanting peaceful things. Where sooner or later the police would come and spray them with water and throw tear gas. But once in a while, recess gave birth to a moment of satisfaction. Even back then I knew what impotence was and that was my goal with this boy. I didn't think he should be able to pass on his toxic genes.

I took off in a sprint laughing, his friends just behind me.

"Get back here you nigger bitch!"

"We're gonna pulverize ya, ya monkey!"

But I knew recess was almost over. All I had to do was make it to where the recess monitor lady usually stationed herself and I'd be safe. I also knew I could outrun all the boys. And if they cornered me, I'd kick my way out. The way my legs carried me as I ran, I must have looked as if I was going for a leisurely jog. But I was moving fast, fast, fast.

I threw my head back and cackled until my lungs burned. And then I cackled some more. Hee hee heeeeee!

• • •

I awoke.

It was a decade later. May. Nineteen ninety-three. I didn't know what day it was. The last date I remembered was the eighteenth.

I looked around the hospital room and shuddered. Fluorescent pink-and-green praying mantises and grass-hoppers were bounding and flying around my bed, clicking and snipping. They were enormous, even bigger than the ones I caught in Nigeria. Directly across from me, a large crow was throwing itself against the window, trying to get inside. With each smack, it lost more oily black feathers. *Window? Where am I*, I thought, barely able to raise my throbbing head.

I glanced around as best I could. There was an ugly yellow chair on my right, pushed against the wall. A large praying mantis was bouncing on the seat's cushion. A boxy television was mounted near the ceiling. It was off. Something clung to my right wrist.

Oh my God, my back surgery is done, I realized. *The countdown is on.*

According to my doctor, in a few weeks I'd be back on the tennis courts with my team, blasting tennis balls down the throats of my opponents, my straight spine snapping backward and then forward each time I hit the ball, as a normal spine should, the fresh scar running down my back hidden beneath my sweaty T-shirt. Then I'd go visit the track and field coach and see if I could join that team instead because I'd always known that that was where I truly belonged. I was finally going to do all the things I loved and I was going to do them as a normal person.

I twitched and felt a dull pang ripple from my spine. The pain was distant, despite its sharpness. I glanced at a large pink-and-green grasshopper perched on my covered legs. I lay back and all these epically important near-future plans stopped mattering. I heard something shatter in the distance and then I was falling back down. I was tumbling backward, head over heels, my long legs tangling. I was falling and tumbling to a place and time where I could run fast and jump high, easily . . .

I was always running. Wednesday, in the Chicago suburb of South Holland, Illinois, 1982, a day like any other.

I was running fast, close on the heels of my two older sisters, Ngozi and Ifeoma. I was breathing harder than normal because

I was terrified. I flew past uniform homes of red, brown, white bricks; green-wire and white-painted wood fences that were recently installed around houses and backyards; and white Ford Mustangs and Nissan Datsuns with black racing stripes. And once in a while there was an empty lot full of weeds. During more peaceful moments, when I wasn't being chased by a group of young racists, I would traipse around in these places looking for nature's beasts.

The light green bulbous spittlebugs were easy to locate. They lived in a dollop of saliva-like fluid. When they grew up, they became insects resembling deep green or sometimes rainbow-colored leafhoppers. So lovely. My favorite creatures were the chunky, fat-butted red-legged grasshoppers and the vibrant green katydids. These were always a treasure because they were hard to spot, let alone catch. There were also bumbling ladybugs, wriggling caterpillars, busy butterflies and moths, tunneling earthworms, and sometimes pinching crayfish, grumpy toads, and slippery frogs. I avoided the sneaky spiders. My father always liked to hear about my day's catch. He too enjoyed witnessing nature up close. Unfortunately, because he was always on call at the hospital, he had to hear about my day's catch late at night, long after I'd freed the creatures.

Nonetheless, at the moment, I wasn't at peace. I wasn't where I wanted to be at all. It was the middle of summer, eighty-five degrees, not a cloud in the sky. The sun shone brightly on exactly what was happening below. I wore pink shorts, a rose-colored shirt, and white Keds. My legs and arms were long and lanky, and children at school called me Palm Tree, Nnedi Spaghetti, and Daddy Longlegs, among other less savory things.

"We're gonna get you, niggeeeeeers!"

Ifeoma was ten, Ngozi was nine, and I was eight. All the kids chasing us were high schoolers. The three of us had just rounded a corner on our way home from the park when we met the group of white kids. My sisters and I froze as we stared at the seven, eight kids. It was a profound moment of realization. All our schedules were about to change.

The white kids were no longer going to talk shit to each other for the next fifteen minutes about why the Scorpions rocked harder than Ratt, and my sisters and I were no longer going to take the short way home. Without a word, the three of us took off. Ifeoma leading, then Ngozi, then me. Our shiny Jheri curls dripped oil and sweat into our eyes. I was sure in my stride, so I snuck a glance back. We would outrun them, though we were much younger. Speed ran in our family.

We ran down the suburban Chicago sidewalks of 1982, like those relatives before us who happily ran down the dirt roads of Isiekenesi and Arondizuogu in Nigeria on their way to the market or school or wherever they were rushing to, like those of my stolen relatives who ran for their lives through the forests and swamps of the United States, and so the cycle continues.

My family was one of the first black families to move into the neighborhood and there was a heavy price to pay for this. They threw paint into our swimming pool, sent letters of hate to our mailbox, shouted "Niggers go home!" as they passed in their cars. Constant harassment.

Nevertheless, neither my sisters nor I thought much about it. It all came with the territory. And being the daughters of confident, academically gifted immigrant doctors from Nigeria, we were taught that all ailments—physical and otherwise—could be worked with, if not cured, taught to always walk with our heads up and to look a scary thing in its many eyes. My parents were essentially healers, their jobs were to make people feel okay, and their kids were not exceptions. Their words were like vitamins to us.

"Just because someone thinks something does not make it true," my mother always said. My parents knew this well, for they came to the United States in 1969, during a time when black people were still believed to be essentially lazy, unambitious, and slow-minded. They came with nothing, ignored these words and sentiments, and did their thing, which included earning a PhD (my mother) and an MD (my father) and bringing four children into the world. No, my parents knew better than to go by old American "truths."

As we ran, something told Ifeoma to make a sharp left between two houses and Ngozi and I quickly followed. It was a dead end. We stopped and turned to face the group. Adrenaline surged from my head to my legs. I was alive and damn ready to fight. I was lanky, but that didn't matter. I'd just about had enough of this bullshit.

It had been like this almost every day. We were always running. The minute we got off the bus, we were running from white folk. We'd be walking around the block and the next minute we were running from white folk. On the playground. Everywhere.

Something had to give. And so, in that dead end we'd been chased into, as the three of us stood facing the enemy, I balled up a fist.

"Where're you little monkeys gonna run now?!" Michelle Ryan sang. The other kids grinned uneasily. They had never caught their prey and they weren't sure what to do now that they had us. But I saw their hands, which were clenched and shaking. And I saw the look in their eyes that broadcast group violence. This was bad. My sisters and I were outnumbered, outweighed, out-aged, and most of them were boys. There was only a moment to decide what to do. I noted the tall leggy blond boy to the left.

The three of us acted at the same time. I moved forward and my sisters moved backward. I lunged and dove right through the blond boy's legs, jumped to my feet, and took off. Behind me, Ngozi and Ifeoma scaled the fence and were gone. The group stood there, indecisive for a beat about whom to chase before just giving up.

I ran and ran. Past houses, empty lots, cars, and driveways. Rounded the corner and ran some more. As fast as my legs would take me. And when I got home, I ran through the door my sisters had left open for me.

Now, I felt another, deeper sense of doneness. Something was finished. Something was broken. Something was hurting. Badly. The pain was deeper than anything I'd ever experienced. So painful that I couldn't even pinpoint where it was coming from. Things were melting together and falling apart. I didn't want to come up the well, but I did. I found a strong foothold and started climbing.

Hospital bed. I groaned. I opened my eyes. It was time to get up.

I couldn't get up.

I examined my surroundings. The room smelled sterile, like many lives had passed through it. I tried to get up again, but I was too tired. I couldn't keep my eyes open. There was clicking and beeping and pain. Time and space were muddy. My joints were stiff. In the back of my mind warning lights flashed red. I felt like a rusted robot. A machine with no waterproofing caught out in the rain, with no shelter nearby. No options. Vulnerable. I was now malfunctioning. I needed a hard reset.

4 The Portal

I awoke gagging, a roughness like sand in my mouth. I tasted something bitter and gagged again. Then, slowly, I looked around. Fluorescent pink-and-green grasshoppers and praying mantises buzzed and flew about the room, loitered at the edge of my hospital bed, climbed up the walls. They rhythmically clicked and snipped.

The crow was now in my room, picking the insects off one by one. I touched the backside of a grasshopper next to my arm on my bedcover and felt the powerful flick of its legs as it hopped off. The sun was shining in, making me squint. I yawned and on reflex started to stretch. Knives of pain pierced me all over.

"Oh, ah, ow!" I hissed. For the first time I paused and looked down at the blanket that covered my legs. It was tan, thin, fuzzy, and ugly. I tried to kick it off. Nothing. I tried again. Nothing. I frowned. It had to be the drugs. Morphine. There was an IV taped to my left wrist and inserted into the vein; its tube ran into a machine to my right. In my right hand was a gray device with a button on top. With each jab of pain, my finger automatically pressed the button. How I knew that doing so administered more morphine, I could not recall.

I tried kicking the blanket off again. Nothing. I blinked. *Weird*, I thought. *My legs have probably already pushed the blanket onto the floor. I'm just seeing something different, or time's slowed? Drugs are so bad. Especially morphine.* I pressed the button again.

"Nnedi." My mother's softly accented voice filled the room.

"Hi, mom," I croaked, my voice husky, my throat dry. A grasshopper landed on her shoulder. My mind was so foggy that I had to fight to keep my eyes open and focus on her face. Never had I seen my mother with such heavy bags under her eyes, eyes that were so red. She hadn't slept and she'd clearly been crying. But why? Her normally perfect large Afro was in rare poor form, slightly lopsided. My father followed her into the room.

"How do you feel?" My father was of one of those African bloodlines that produced men with lion voices. "Have you eaten?"

"No. I'm not hungry."

"Doesn't matter, you still need to eat something," my father boomed. "Keeps you strong."

My sister Ngozi and my best friend, James, walked in next. I'd instantly become friends with James in my first year of college. The sight of his smile always made me smile—the perfect white of his grin contrasted strikingly with the rich brown of his skin. Today, though, he struggled to smile. "We brought you a Sausage McMuffin with egg and two hash browns," he said.

"*And* a giant Dove bar, milk chocolate," Ngozi added.

My twelve-year-old brother, Emezie, walked in, silent. He took a seat in the yellow chair, never taking his eyes off me.

"No . . . I . . . I'm not hungry," I said, speaking slowly to avoid slurring my words. I was uncomfortable with everyone crowding into the room. Only Ifeoma was absent, still in South America on a school trip. I was glad she didn't have to see me like this. A skeleton under a blanket. The crow on the windowsill cawed and no one else seemed to hear it. Nor did they hear all the clicking and snipping of the radioactive-looking grasshoppers and praying mantises.

My father put his hand on my chest and said, "Take a deep breath."

I could only manage a shallow one. Me, the one who could run four hundred meters in one minute with next to no training. Everyone was staring at me. I understood why. I'd have stared too.

"How ya doin', kiddo?" The doctor entered the room. I wanted to frown, but instead I stared into his blue eyes. Like my mother's, they were weighed down with bags and bloodshot. I urgently wanted everyone to leave. There was something slippery sliding around in my mind and I couldn't concentrate on it unless I was alone.

"Fine, I guess," I mumbled.

Satisfied, he stepped out, and I took the opportunity to confess. "I keep . . . seeing things."

James rubbed his shiny head and glanced at my sister. She

was biting her black-painted nails. My brother didn't move. My mother frowned. My dad leaned forward.

"Like what?" he asked.

"I dunno, like bugs and stuff," I whispered. "And things like that. Creepy creatures or whatever."

"Bugs?" my father asked, his eyebrows rising. He only got that look when we talked about insects. My love of nature had been planted and cultivated by him. My father was fascinated by nature's oddities: plants with sophisticated nervous systems, flooded forests, glowing fish, perfectly camouflaged insects, electric eels, birds that could imitate the call of many birds at once. He introduced me to *Nova* and National Geographic animal programs and we often watched them together.

Instantly, I felt a little better. His look reminded me that all was not chaos. So I began to tell him all about my insect-filled visions.

The surgeon stepped back into the room.

"How long will she be on the morphine?" my mother asked.

"Well, when the pain subsides a bit . . ."

"Put her on codeine," my father said.

"We don't want her to become addicted," my mother added.

It's a very good thing to have parents who are both doctors.

"We'll take her off the morphine in a day or so," he said with a nod. I felt a sting of annoyance. What was codeine? Were the painkilling effects weaker than what they had me on?

"Hang in there," my father said, squeezing my shoulder.

"Bye," my brother said. He wasn't very tall yet, but his feet were huge. He was awkward and gangly like a young German shepherd, all potential. James slapped my hand and grasped it, flashing me that smile, looking like a young black Mr. Clean. He handed me the small tape player he'd bought me.

"There's a mix tape in there," he said.

Ngozi gave me a light hug. "We'll be back tomorrow," she said. "Call whenever."

My mother leaned forward, put her hand on my arm, and kissed my cheek. When I looked where her hand had been, I saw and felt a warm reddish-brown handprint. I heard the door close. I was alone again. With my muddled thoughts and ethereal creatures. I pressed Play on the tape player. First song, PM Dawn, "Looking Through Patient Eyes." It was just what I needed. My room went a warm, gentle blue and swirled with the sound.

Over the next few hours time stretched, twisted, and shrank. I watched the sun rise. Then set. Then rise again. Then set. It rose and set some more and I woozily gazed through it all.

• • •

Five years ago. In my father's village of Arondizuogu. The town that was the origin of so much for me. Walking with my sisters down the red dirt road, sneezing in the dust sent into the air by passing cars, coughing whenever an exhaust-belching car passed.

Biting into the warm sticky mango in my hand between coughs.

It was Christmas Day and we'd just gotten back from the most intense, ridiculous church service ever: people singing way too loudly, shouting to Jesus, the women wearing huge, colorful gele. The church was so hot that everyone was sweating freely, and there was the sound of chickens fighting nearby during the quietest parts of the service.

My sisters and I were walking from a cousin's house when we rounded the concrete corner of a dusty unfinished house. "Raaaaahhhhhhh!" A masquerade leapt from behind the wall, all straw, raffia, and multiple ebony faces. Masquerades were physical manifestations of the spirits and ancestors, all in the form of boys or men in elaborate costumes. We screamed as it danced wildly before us, undulating and shaking its hips. I stood there staring, my mouth an O of terror and fascination, the image of this fantastical beast in real life burned into my mind forever. Then we turned and took off. It gave chase.

Down the dirt road we all sprinted: Ifeoma, then Ngozi, then me, then the creature that was supposed to be a spirit or ancestor personified who was out to spend Christmas Day with human beings. We zoomed past my parents, who were sitting on my aunt's porch sipping orange Fanta (my mother) and STAR lager (my father). They noted us and then went back to whatever conversation they were having. Eventually, my sisters and I outran the masquerade and for the rest of the trip we bragged that we outran the spirits that day.

You can't, however, outrun your ancestors.

I sighed, wondering if I'd ever outrun anything again. And what I wouldn't have given for a visit from the ancestors right at that moment, so they could tell me what the hell to do. I decided to focus on the grasshoppers and praying mantises if only not to see the beginning and end of yet another day.

5 White Coats

I opened my eyes and my heart dropped. Still these four walls. I hadn't been outside in three days; I could feel it in my skin. The summer was beginning out there. The earth was breathing and sprouting and expanding. But I was in a hospital room withering.

I stretched my arms and sighed. Then I froze, a frown on my face as my eyes fell on a doctor in a white coat entering the room, followed by another and another and another and another and . . . was this the morphine again? No. The IV was still in the vein on my left hand, but the morphine cart was gone. My mind was clearer than it had been in days. Grasshoppers and praying mantises have short life spans. They must have died. The crow must have flown out the window, finally having had its fill. But who were all these people standing in my hospital room?

"Good morning, Nnedi," my surgeon said. Behind him stood seven other people in matching white coats. "How are you feeling?"

I paused as a random thought passed through my mind: *Why haven't I had to go to the bathroom?* There was a moment.

A millisecond. I was floating in the blackness of space. There was breathless silence. Metallic disconnect.

Stop.

I caught it; that elusive thought that had hopped, pranced, and skipped from my conscious hands. I gripped it hard enough, hoping to squeeze it to death. Of course, it didn't die. Facts don't die. It had happened. *There was a one percent chance*, I thought. *It happened*. I tried to move my legs. Nothing. *The unthinkable has happened*. I was paralyzed. I couldn't move my legs. I couldn't get out of bed. Even if the room were filling with giant black dirt-covered wolf spiders, I couldn't get up. My eye twitched.

I like to imagine that the night before my surgery, the doctor took his wife to a restaurant and they feasted on crab legs, chicken legs, frog legs, and rice pilaf. That would explain a lot of things. If he chowed down on frog legs and crab legs and chicken legs the night before performing surgery on me, maybe as his teeth crushed their cooked flesh, deviant ideas about the surgery he would perform the next day on a young woman materialized and bounced into his subconscious. He was a good man and a good doctor, so I doubt those ideas were conscious.

I glanced at my surgeon and all the other white coats and shuddered. I wanted them all to get the fuck out of my room. He smiled warmly at me. "Looks like you're pretty famous, Nnedi," he said. The bags still hung heavily beneath his bloodshot eyes. Now I knew why. He'd been crying and losing sleep, just like my mother. I wanted to punch him in the face and make his eyes more bloodshot with fresh blood and swelling. But I couldn't get up. I broke into a sweat. My surgeon gestured around the room. "These are residents whom I've told about what's happened to you. It's rare that this happens to someone in as good of shape as you. We'll want to watch you closely."

"Yeah . . . yeah, sure." I rubbed my hand down my face, muttering, "Oh my God."

"Can you feel anything in your legs yet?"

Stop.

In that moment I went mad. Seconds stretched and tore at the seams and between those ragged folds of time, I burst from my body, through the ceiling, through the floors above me, into the sky, my fists clenched, my neck veins throbbing, my teeth bared, my mouth wide. I screamed, my mouth expanding to the size of a hurricane eye, which began furiously rotating and inside that eye was chaos and destruction. Then I was sucked back down into my body. My unmoving body. Rage contained.

My surgeon didn't notice a thing. Neither did the residents standing behind him. The room should have looked as though a tornado had ripped through it. Everyone's hair should have been blown about. Some of the residents should have been dead, dashed violently against the battered walls. Instead, they all stood there smiling pleasantly at me, studying me, taking in my details, yet missing the most vital ones. They'd all assumed I knew about my condition from the moment I woke up. But how *could* I have with all those hallucinations? I'd been around friends who'd taken all kinds of drugs and drank all sorts of alcohol, but I'd never even been drunk before.

"No," I said, only a slight tremor in my voice. "I . . . I can't move them at all." Some of the residents wrote this down.

I felt nothing from the waist down. At about my belly button, there was tingling when I touched the flesh there, but beyond that perimeter was an abyss. It was as if half of me had teleported to another dimension. Probably one where I had a straight spine and an athletic career.

"Well, you *look* okay. Don't worry," he said. Then he smiled. To my eyes, his smile was sheepish and dripping with guilt, doubt, and dishonesty. He had no idea whether I would walk again.

The white coats filed out of the room, and when I heard the door close, I tried to move my legs again. Nothing. I tried and tried and tried. I felt grungy, as if toxins were building up inside me from lack of movement. Sweat formed on my forehead and I grew dizzy and more fatigued. I grabbed the edge of the covers and flicked them back and stared at my legs.

Two brown sticks.

At least my legs were still there. I was wearing a pink hospital gown that went halfway down my thighs; from there, it was miles of bare, useless legs and then ugly tan socks. I couldn't bring my legs up to check, but I had a feeling the socks were the type with the traction on the bottom. Socks made for people who could walk. My skin was chapped and that made me want to cry some more. I did.

Another wave of dizziness washed over me and I could hear my pulse in my ears. "Oh God, no no no," I sobbed, pounding a fist into the pillow. Even this was weak. I wanted to run. Out of the room. Out of my body. *I'm broken*, I thought. *Oh my God, I'm really, really broken.*

I tried to roll to my side to get more comfortable and couldn't. I needed the use of my hips to do that. My legs looked so thin. How quickly one's muscle mass decreases when the muscles aren't used. I could see the tiny hairs on them. They'd need a good shave in a week. Could I even do that? A rush of pain flew through me. For the first time I could identify where the pain was coming from. My back.

Days ago, my surgeon and his medical team had sliced me open, grasped my twisted spine, unknowingly straightened it to the point of paralyzing me, realized I couldn't move my legs, gone back in and decreased the straightening, fused several of my vertebrae, then lashed a stainless steel rod to it to hold it in place, then sewn me up. During all that, this beast of pain was born. Unhindered by morphine, this fiery beast writhed and roiled.

"I'll get better," I muttered. Still, it was clear that my surgeon wasn't telling me everything. It was in his sleep-deprived eyes, his tentative body language. The quiver at the corner of his mouth. Regardless, if I could conquer pain, I could conquer other things. Bigger, worse things. I had conquered tough things on the tennis court and the track. I told myself that had all just been practice for this moment.

An hour later, I didn't feel so confident. I broke down, not fifty percent, not ninety-nine percent, but one hundred percent. Into pieces. My head tumbled into a corner, my torso rolled under the bed, my legs stacked on the floor, my potential track career vanished into thin air, my tennis career bounced into the trash, and my happiness moldered into the rotten gray color of depression. I'd become a Frida Kahlo painting.

At the time, I couldn't see past my broken self. However, when I look back, considering Frida's lifelong struggle with her body and what that struggle opened into probably would have given me some much-needed perspective and strength. Frida Kahlo was a Mexican painter who is most known for her self-portraits and ability to paint her pain into beauty.

Much of Kahlo's work centers on broken bodies, most often her own. In her painting *The Broken Column*, Frida paints her spine in a way that accentuates its disintegrating state and just how much pain she was in because of it. It's exposed to the elements. Instead of bone, her spine is made of crumbling stone. Nails have been pounded into her body, from her face, to her arms, to her chest and torso.

Many speculate that Frida was born with spina bifida, a condition that causes defects in the spinal cord and vertebrae, which can lead to limited mobility, bladder and bowel problems, infections, and yes, scoliosis. What's known for certain about her physical hardships is that she contracted polio at age six and was in a trolley accident at eighteen. This accident left her with a broken spine, a broken pelvis, and a pierced abdomen. It was while laid up in bed, trying to recover, that her parents encouraged her to paint. Eventually Frida recovered, but for the rest of her short life (she died at age forty-seven), she suffered from chronic pain.

Knowing this, I view *The Broken Column* through a skewed lens. Where Frida wants me to see her suffering and anguish, I also see a woman who has become more because of that suffering and anguish. I don't see a stone column for a spine; I see a column of steel. The cracks in it make her more flexible. I don't see nails; I see sensors that detect the world around her, bringing her more information than any purely organic human being. I see a cyborg.

Frida's Breaking did not break her. In fact, it was *because* of all the pain she transcended that she made beautiful art that still moves the souls of many today.

"Feet, what do I need you for when I have wings to fly?"

—Frida Kahlo

• • •

Come nightfall, after my family visited and had gone home, I was left with myself—what was left of me. I was sinking into a cold, syrupy darkness. I sat there staring at the wall, my legs stretched before me. On the small shelf right beside my head were the old, worn, mass market–sized science fiction anthologies and short story collections James had brought me. I glanced at them skeptically. There were spaceships, robots, and alien worlds on the covers. I was more into horror writers like Stephen King, Robert McCammon, and Clive Barker. Plus, I was too distracted and in too much pain to read anything. Instead, I tumbled down the rabbit hole . . .

Days ago I could do anything. What if the wound on my back gets infected? I wish time travel were real. Why won't anyone answer the call buzzer? The night nurses don't care. I'm alone. Maybe my arms will stop working next. They don't know what's happening anyway, so why can't anything just happen? No escape. It happened already. I can't go back. What if the hospital catches on fire? If the soul really is connected and dependent on the body, I'm fucked. I'll always be deformed. I'm deformed. What am I? Who am I if I can't run?

6 I Made Her From Clay

The praying mantises were back. They hopped high into the air, propelling themselves easily with their strong green legs. They clicked past my face. Thousands of them. I sat in my bed, unable to run away. I was being buried in arthropodic limbs, thoraxes, wings, triangular heads. My legs were covered with flying and crawling insects, moving up my waist. They were making their way up farther still. I screeched, brushing away the ones I could reach. I shivered, moments away from panic. Again. I started to gag . . .

I awoke with a start, my throat clenching and unclenching, my stomach convulsing. My mind grabbed at its surroundings. The chair, the TV quietly playing soft music (Janet Jackson's "That's the Way Love Goes"), the sealed window. Oriented now, I began to settle, but the feeling of complete disgust lingered. My face was frozen in a grimace, though I wasn't exactly sure why. I'd been in the hospital for a week and a half now and this was the fourth time I'd awakened from a vivid, strange dream, gagging. I hated codeine. "It's milder than morphine, but it can give some people bad dreams," my father said when I'd asked him yesterday if codeine had hallucinatory effects. "Some people." People like me.

Because I couldn't wheel myself very far into the rest of the hospital to visit with people my age, that afternoon I sat with several young children as they did arts and crafts. Picking up a piece of blue clay, I began molding a long-legged woman. I used Popsicle sticks for her legs and rolled seven long thin chunks for her hair. In my mind, they were dreadlocks. Something told me to give her large breasts and I did this without question, knowing to trust and follow my creative process from the start. I hadn't come up with a name for her yet but I knew it would be a name Americans would find difficult to pronounce. I smiled, something I hadn't done in a while.

The little boy beside me was making a truck and the little girl on my other side was just mashing the clay with her fist. The IV bag she carted around sat behind her, and I worried about the IV in her forearm falling out as she pounded. I liked being around these children. Their energy, no matter how depleted, was positive and shiny and sometimes I could talk smiles onto their faces. We had a lot in common. We liked to watch cartoons, play video games, and we were all incapacitated in some way.

Sitting up in the wheelchair was not easy to do for extended periods of time. It always grew uncomfortable, as it did now. But at least I had my clay lady. And she was special, I was sure of it. Knowing this somehow lessened the pain as I wheeled myself back to my room.

But by the time I got there, I was gasping for breath, swallowing back screams of pain. The pain medication would work for several hours, but when it ran out, it was always sudden. The beast I'd come to know so well was squirming stealthily just beneath the surface. Watching, waiting, brooding behind a veil. Then when it got its chance, it broke through, teeth bared, claws out, breath of fire.

I grasped the doorknob with a quivering, sweaty hand. As I wheeled in, my toe hit the side of the door so hard my leg was nearly knocked from the footrest. I couldn't focus my mind enough to worry about it. I pressed the call button for the nurses to help me into bed and fought to keep my spirit from fleeing my body to somewhere more peaceful.

Once on the bed, I sat there clutching the clay lady. The nurse said he'd be back with more pain medication, so in that moment, the beast of pain was wrapped tightly around my body and looking over my shoulder with a hot grin, its cold saliva dribbling down my shoulder onto my chest. I dumped the clay lady on top of the stack of books on the small shelf beside me.

I reached for a book from the stack, just to distract myself from the pain, and hissed as the slight motion burst like fire along my back. I clutched the book and cracked it open. Over and over, I read the first few sentences, but I just couldn't concentrate. The pain's squeeze was fogging my senses. There was a pen on the shelf. A nurse must have left it there. I grabbed it. In high school, when the drone of certain teachers became unbearable I used to doodle. Focusing on the motion of the pen and the drawing of lines always pulled me out of my boredom, making me more able to listen to the teacher.

This time was different. I didn't draw loops, swirls, crosses, or squiggles. I didn't obsess over how closely I could draw lines around each other without letting them touch. I didn't practice drawing three-dimensional cubes or cylinders. I drew letters and strung them together into words, then sentences, then a paragraph. The sensation was like this:

A door opened, and with it came a warm breeze.
The breath of a beast. It was the sky.
There it was.
I grasped it.
My ancestors laughed.
Because finally, I'd found it.

I drew the clay lady, except she actually wasn't made of clay. She was flesh and bone, tall, with strange dreadlocks that crept down her back. She had a severe face. She wore a long blue dress, like something a nun would wear. It went all the way to her neck, down to her wrists, and was so long that it covered her big feet. She lived in a small village in Nigeria. A long time ago. I didn't know how she wasn't all sweaty in that dress. "Oh," I said, as I scribbled all this around the edges of *I, Robot*. "I know why she's not hot in that dress. Not all the time, at least." This woman could fly.

I looked up and blinked, realizing something. I still felt the pain, clutching me as tightly as ever, its weight pressing me down. It was so bad that I was squinting my eyes, tears were rolling down my face, my mouth hung open, and I was gripping the pen so hard that my double-jointed fingers bent in crazy directions. And yet, under that weight and compression, something in me aligned, focused, opened.

Reveling in this new sensation, I went back in . . . or should I say *out*? If this woman I'd just created had the ability to fly, then that meant she could fly out of my hospital room whenever she wanted. "Legs? What do I need them for?" she'd say as she flew through my hospital room window, into the warm night sky on her way to wherever she wanted to go. I gazed from the words I'd scribbled to the clay lady and back to the words. I felt greater than myself. I felt myself become greater.

• • •

My creation of the clay lady reminds me of the speculations about Mary Shelley and the inspiration for her novel *Frankenstein*, which is believed to be *the* first science fiction novel. The child of parents who were both authors and political philosophers, Mary Shelley was born and raised in a deeply intellectual household. In her introduction to the 1831 edition of the text, she wrote, "It is not singular that, as the daughter of two persons of distinguished literary celebrity, I should very early in life have thought of writing. As a child I scribbled; and my favourite pastime, during the hours given me for recreation, was to 'write stories.' "

So early on, writing and viewing the world with perceptive eyes was a part of Shelley's upbringing. Intellect deepened into profound creativity when darker elements of life experience were mixed in.

The origin story of *Frankenstein* typically goes like this: In the late spring of 1816, known as the "Year Without a Summer," when Mary was eighteen years old, she and a small group of friends (including Lord Byron and Percy Shelley) gathered in Geneva, Switzerland, and stayed in a villa near Lake Geneva. (This was the year after the volcanic eruption of Mount Tambora, which spewed smoke, sulfuric rock, ash, and fumes so far that temperatures worldwide were dramatically lower the next year.) The weather was poor and they were forced to spend a lot of time indoors, where they told ghost stories to one another. Lord Byron later suggested they have a ghost story–writing contest. It was Mary's resulting short story that gave birth to *Frankenstein*.

However, it may not have just been a flash of genius that inspired her. There is speculation that it may have been childbirth. Her mother died less than two weeks after giving birth to her, Mary herself had previously endured the death of a child she'd given birth to prematurely, and if the timeline is accurate, Shelley was pregnant when she wrote *Frankenstein*. In the novel, the scientist creates unnatural life and it runs amok. It's not hard to see the connections.

Those connections grow even clearer on closer inspection. Ruth Franklin, writing in *The New Republic*, recounts a particularly telling moment: "'I have no doubt of seeing the animal today,' Mary Wollstonecraft wrote hastily to her husband,

William Godwin, on August 30, 1797, as she waited for the midwife who would help her deliver the couple's first child. The 'animal' was Mary Wollstonecraft Godwin, who would grow up to be Mary Shelley."[1] In *Frankenstein*, the scientist refers to the monster he creates in the same way, as "the animal."

Could it be that Mary wrote *Frankenstein* as a way of facing her pain and fears? That she produced something so great and beyond herself from the grief she suffered? If this is true, then not only did Mary Shelley have her own "clay lady" (Frankenstein's monster), but an entire genre of literature (science fiction) was launched by the Breaking.

---

[1] Ruth Franklin, "Was 'Frankenstein' Really About Childbirth?", *The New Republic*, March 7, 2012, https://newrepublic.com/article/101435/mary-shelley-frankenstein-godwin-bodleian-oxford.

7 Twitch

Summer was passing me by. Somewhere out there the birds were singing, a warm breeze was blowing, sunflowers were getting tall enough to start growing their huge seedy heads. And all I could do was sit in that bed and watch it go.

Then I felt a sudden itch in my left leg. An uncontrollable pang. As if one of those damn praying mantises was crawling across my ankle. My left big toe twitched. Just like that. I hadn't even been trying to do anything in that moment. Two days before, my physical therapist had asked me to try to move my toe and the effort left me drenched with sweat, result-free.

Now I felt woozy with surprise and hope. Even if I hadn't willed it, my toe had moved. It was no longer dead. Its soul had returned, but was it only for a moment? I had to recapture it completely before it fled again. I was sure I only had seconds. I stared at my toe now, my heart pounding hard in my chest.

My toe was an organism separate from myself. It was unpredictable, temperamental, shy, and my life depended on it. My toe twitched again. An animal trying to get my attention. Oh it certainly had my attention now. I gave it the fullest, sharpest, most inspired attention I'd ever mustered. I focused on that toe. I willed and willed it to twitch a third time. I knew it could *hear* what I asked of it, but it didn't have to obey. So I asked and asked, "Big toe, please, kindly, twitch again. For me. You just did it on your own. You can do it again. You know you want to. I'll forever keep you well scrubbed and your nail painted with pretty colors. I'll rub you with rose oil. And if I ever have a boyfriend, I'll make him kiss you three times each night."

This was my *Kill Bill* moment. In *Kill Bill: Volume 1*, the revenge-driven assassin Beatrix Kiddo has to awaken her atrophied legs after being in a coma for four years. She sits in the back seat of a small truck and while looking at her feet calmly recites over and over, "Wiggle your big toe." In a story about taking revenge against everyone who wronged her, this is a rare instance where Beatrix can't use her physical strength and has to instead consult her mental and spiritual abilities in order to go on.

After hours of mentally coaxing her toes, then feet, then legs into functioning, she is able to continue her violent spree of revenge. Though this is fantasy (muscle atrophy is far from merely being a state of mind and requires months of intense physical therapy), there is still a powerful lesson in Beatrix's struggle. For the first time, due to a terrible incident (being shot in the head), Beatrix has to be something she would have never been otherwise: She has to be still. In this stillness, she is forced to rediscover and then use mental skills she's forgotten because of the hatred clouding her mind. The lessons she learns from this moment of forced staticity would save her life later on and make her a far greater warrior.

Twitch.

"Ah, thank you," I sighed with a grin.

I asked my toe to twitch again. And again and again. And my toe didn't tire of my requests, as long as I was polite. Later on that day, the same sweet treatment worked on my right big toe. After a hard reset, the reboot had *finally* truly begun.

• • •

Slowly but steadily my legs came back from where they'd gone. On Tuesday, I didn't feel a thing. On Wednesday, there was tingling. On Sunday, I couldn't curl my foot. On Monday, I could curl it ever so slightly. On Wednesday, I couldn't lift my leg while sitting in my wheelchair. On Friday, I could lift it just enough for it to jerk and slip off the footrest. Through it all, I pushed myself in physical therapy as if I was training for an epic tennis match until the day finally came where I sat in my chair in front of those shiny cold bars.

There was a mirror in front of the bars, facing me. The better to let your eyes compensate for what your legs couldn't do. The doctors and physical therapists called it proprioception, the ability to know where your body parts were through nerve messages of touch and balance. It's what allows you to walk or run without looking at your feet.

Because of the nerve damage I'd suffered from the spinal surgery, my sense of proprioception was next to nothing. I couldn't always tell where my legs were in space. I'd somehow become more suited to move through water or in antigravity than on land. If I didn't live on a planet with gravity, this wouldn't have been as much of a problem. The irony of my paralysis making me—a future science fiction writer—better suited for outer space than Earth was lost on me back then.

I had tried to stand days earlier, but my legs simply couldn't lift me up. It was scarier than anything I had done so far—there was a risk of falling that could result in further injury. The sensation in my legs was returning, but standing was still like standing on semi-invisible objects that weren't quite a part of my body. "You basically have to learn to walk again," my physical therapist, Siedah, had said.

Easy for her to say. As with most people, Siedah didn't remember learning how to walk. And it was something she would probably not have to go through again. Now, sitting in my wheelchair before those bars again, pushing my frustration aside, I settled and prepared myself to do something simple yet incredible—something I'd never known I'd be able to do, something I'd never thought I'd ever *have* to do: teach my adult body how to walk.

• • •

Back then I had no examples of people who had succeeded in relearning how to use their bodies. Since my own relearning, I've found several such stories, and they never cease to astound me. All of them are incredible in their own unique way. One of the most stunning examples I've recently come across is Hugh Herr.

When I learned about Hugh Herr's journey I both laughed loudly and cried. Then I just stared into space imagining the possibilities, thinking, "This is how it begins." Hugh Herr is an engineer who, after losing his lower legs due to a perilous mountain climbing situation, went on to create super-advanced bionic limbs that emulate the function of natural limbs. Herr is responsible for breakthrough advances in bionic limbs that provide greater mobility and new hope to those with physical disabilities. Herr didn't just teach himself to walk again, he created himself anew, as something beyond who he was before it all happened. Some of his latest designs are even starting to incorporate cyborg elements, including the connection of bionic hardware to human nervous systems.

The prosthetic limbs he created allowed him to return to climbing. And not only did he create new legs for himself, those legs turned out to be better than his old ones. He could climb more difficult surfaces and wedge his prosthetic feet into smaller rock fissures. He even found that by adjusting these limbs he could change his height to suit his needs whenever he wanted. Eventually, he began climbing to heights he hadn't been able to climb with his physiological legs, metaphorically and literally.

Herr has said: "I didn't view my body as broken. I reasoned that a human being can never be 'broken.' Technology is broken."

And look what is possible because Herr fixed what was broken (in this case, technology). What moved my soul the most were the robotic exoskeletons he has created. This exoskeleton augments a person's ability to walk; with them, someone who has no trouble walking could be made to walk for miles and miles without getting tired. Herr's creations got me dreaming about running again, *really, truly* running. Running without having to make my brain do quadruple the work telling each leg how to lift, each foot how to land because I lacked the instinct I'd developed as a baby. I dreamed of effortlessly running faster and quicker than I ever could have with the use of my biological legs and uninjured spinal cord. Herr gave me those dreams with his realities.

So . . . In the year 2029, my legs' exoskeletons are made of magnesium alloy woven into a delicate periwinkle lattice of networks, thin and barely noticeable like the web of a spider that catches the light just so. They move with my body and yield to my weight as I sit down. But don't be fooled by the delicate appearance, power runs through every thin cord, augmenting my legs with agility. Resting against my back is a paper thin, flexible gel, waterproof pad that would heat, cool, and gently pulse signals that replace the proprioceptive signals I'd lost due to my paralysis. This means that this receptive pad returns my sense of where my legs are in space.

Moving about my world is smooth, normal. People are still intrigued by the exoskeletons and getting through TSA is still a hassle, even with PreCheck, but those are minor things. The constant fear of falling, the numbness, the disappearing is a thing of the past. Walking in the snow is no longer a nightmare. Walking down the street with chatty friends is no longer a grand exercise in concentration. I attend more music concerts because being in crowds no longer feels like being thrown into outer space. I jog around my neighborhood.

Tapping a tiny button near the thin cords at my left ankle causes the exoskeleton to kick into "bionic mode," a mode that triples proprioception and strength augmentation. I can run and jump three times quicker and faster without breaking more than my usual sweat. In this way, I don't have to drive to the teashop and bookstore a few miles away or to make quick trips to the supermarket.

In 2029, I'm anything but normal. I am a cyborg.

• • •

However, in 1993, I wasn't quite there yet. I was closer to where I'd been as an infant, frustrated as I tried to retrain my body to do such a seemingly simple task.

I hoisted myself up.

I looked at the mirror, into my own eyes, and talked to my legs with my mind. *Okay*, I thought. *Please straighten up. Now gently lock your knees. Use your quads and calf muscles. Remember how you used to be. Remember how you used to be. Remember how you used to be.*

I thought of all I'd been through. The nurses with their fake nails and fashion magazines, who took forever to respond to my calls. Sorrow. Enduring constipation because of the iron pills they gave me. My surgeon and all those white-coated residents.

Panic and claustrophobia. Mystical and possibly toxic praying mantises and irate crows. Sticks for legs. An early menstruation due to my body being in shock. Monstrous pain. Then I thought about how badly I wanted to walk and took all these emotions and flooded them into my legs for support. I didn't think about my ancestors who most certainly had been there that day, standing behind me. Giving me strength.

I stood there.

I was standing again.

I brought it all with me back to my hospital room. The distant ache in my awakening legs from muscles I hadn't used in weeks, the shake in my hands from the adrenaline that had washed into my system, the hot, tight pain of the healing scar running down my back, the glowing evidence in my heart that I could and would. I was charged. I was magical. Small yet potent, like a venomous beetle deep in the soil that had just seen a path to the surface, a crack that ran deep. I put all this down on paper, letting it heat my pen.

I stayed up late, whipped up in a small tornado of writing about the woman who could fly and the shadowy man who was always standing behind my hospital bed just out of my sight.

8 Rusting Robot

I remember how I used to be.

On the tennis court, there were days when I could see through time. It happened most often when things got really heated. Something inside me would align. The tennis term for this heightened state of being is "treeing." It is when you are playing out of your mind, when you can do no wrong, when you can make the universe yield to your every whim. I know it sounds intense, because it is. When I treed, sometimes I could predict the future. Not that far, about one second. I'd know exactly where my opponent was going to hit the ball because I'd see it happen right before it did. It was just enough time to make use of the knowledge.

Even before I began to write science fiction, though I didn't know it, I *was* sci-fi.

In those moments, my athleticism really *was* a superpower. Now, when I write about characters with abilities, the gift of flight, time travel, shape-shifting, I draw from my own experiences as an incredible athlete. And for these characters' conflicts and limitations within the narrative, I draw from my experiences with and recovering from paralysis.

• • •

The next step was relearning how to walk, and this was best done in the water first. Getting each of my legs through their respective holes in the bathing suit was difficult. Nonetheless, I was tired of being naked in front of nurses, so I struggled through. I sat on my hospital bed and bent my legs to my chest as far as they would go, until my knees were touching my face. Then, carefully, I slipped the left foot in. It took several attempts. My legs kept slipping forward and I kept almost falling to the side. Once I got the bathing suit on, I tried to ignore how frail my body looked.

I wheeled myself to the edge of the small pool where my physical therapist Siedah and her student assistant, Banali, were waiting, also in bathing suits. This was my third time at the pool. The first two times they sat me on the edge and had me paddle my legs. I had kicked and kicked, slowly, but enough to break a sweat. I felt well exercised afterward. The endorphins were pumping. However, just getting me to the rim of the pool was terrifying. If I accidentally pitched forward into the water, I could barely kick my legs. I'd drown easily.

Now, sitting at the edge of the pool between two bars, I stared at the water for several minutes, frozen. I was thinking of collapsing, hitting my head, drowning, reinjuring my healing but still crooked back, the people passing by the huge window in front of me witnessing it all. I was thinking there was no other way. I would never walk again if I didn't take the risks. I thought of percentages and chance.

Finally, I stopped. I submitted, thinking, "What will be will be. Forward. No looking back." I slid in. Banali had to catch me because I couldn't support myself. Banali and Siedah were quiet, letting me build up courage and acclimate myself. Then Siedah said, "All right, Nnedi, let's do this. We're here."

"We won't let you fall," Banali added, holding out her brown hands.

I held the bars, my legs shaking. I held my breath, my eyes wide open. My legs and the buoyancy of the water were supporting me. As long as no one around me moved too much, sloshing the water around and messing with my balance, I was fine. I was standing. I sighed with relief. There it was. That feeling of being able to support my own body. There it was. YES!

Banali came closer and the slight disturbance to the water almost knocked me over. I grasped the bars more tightly.

"You think you can walk a bit?" Siedah asked.

I looked down at my legs. Standing was one thing, but walking was another. I couldn't quite remember what it felt like to walk.

I raise the leg, lean forward, bring it down, I thought. Slowly, I began following my own instructions. And that was how I took my first step. Not the way a baby does it, by instinct, but by mechanics. As a science. I was reading a mental manual on walking as I made myself walk. Banali and Siedah clapped and cheered. I grinned and sighed with relief. That was it for that day. The next day I took three steps. And the next it was seven. By the end of the week, using the bars, I finally walked across the small pool.

A week later, when Siedah presented me with a walker, I stared at it. *That's what old people use*, I thought. *I shouldn't have to use one of those for another eight decades, if ever!*

Lift left leg, step, push; lift right leg, step, push. Every time I pushed, it made a horrible groaning sound, rubber dragging on hospital tile flooring. Almost as bad as scratching a chalk-board with your nails. I felt like a rusting robot. Nevertheless, I was walking. I could move, albeit slowly, around my hospital room. I could go to the bathroom alone. I *was* freer. But just as things were getting better, just as I got used to and more comfortable with my plight, as the habit of writing strange little tales to myself became a part of my life, it was time to change. Again.

It was time to go home.

9 Dammit

The drive home from the hospital was strange. I wondered if it was because I had been there for so long that I'd forgotten what a car felt like. It had only been a month, but occasionally time is relative. Within a month, I'd ended one lifetime and begun another.

I sat in the front seat, my mother driving the brick-red Ford Explorer. I was stiff, my back brace propping me up. Every thump felt like we were going over a speed bump at a hundred miles an hour. My mother's SUV, in which you normally felt like you were flying rather than driving, had become a moving earthquake. I was afraid I'd be shaken apart again.

I didn't want to go home. I didn't want to see the house, my room, the rooms and hallways in which I had pranced about like a gazelle for the last seven years of my life, since we moved from our previous house in South Holland. I was returning as a different person. Slow-moving, thinner, sadder, my head swollen with new experiences.

I didn't want to face any of this.

I still had my track-and-field state meet schedule from the year before tacked to my bedroom wall. The paper number that was pinned to my uniform was still on my dresser. My running shoes, Wilson tennis bag with its four periwinkle Wilson Profile rackets, my blue towel, a half-eaten energy bar, my U of I tennis skirts that always wafted up in the wind when I was hitting a serve.

That other me would be lurking around the house, a confused ghost. She'd have all that energy and nothing to focus it on because her purpose had been cut free and sent spiraling into outer space. All still in my room. The room that it took me fifteen minutes to get to from the garage door that day. I had to walk through the kitchen, down the long hallway, then down the stairs where my room and Ngozi's room were.

The house was three stories, plus a basement. The laundry room, my room, my sister's room, and the family room were on a slightly underground floor. Then there was the ground level, which was most of the house, including the kitchen, expansive computer room, one of the bathrooms, and living room with its high ceilings. Upstairs was where Ifeoma's, Emezie's and my parents' rooms were. It was truly a lovely house, but it was no place for someone who was wheelchair-bound.

When I reached my room, I shakily stood in the middle of it, grasping my walker, looking around as my mother put my stuff away. My mother helped me sit on the bed and then I pulled myself to the far end, so I could rest my brace-encased back against the wall. I sat there and looked around some more.

I blinked and then sighed. My room was cool and had that familiar earthy smell.

When my mother finally stepped out to go get the rest of my things, I took the moment to let myself sink back into this place. This familiar place. With its familiar smells. With its familiar things. With its familiar creaks and groans at night. With its familiar ghosts and spirits. I frowned, resistant. None of this was me anymore. Not the Midnight Oil or Garfield poster on the wall. Or the stack of horror novels on my night table. Or the wooden masks on the wall that I'd bought in Nigeria. Not the Doc Marten boots and flannel shirts in my closet.

I leaned over and grabbed a book off my dresser. It was a hefty mass-market paperback of one of my favorite novels, *The Talisman* by Stephen King and Peter Straub. I'd first read this exact copy when I was twelve and since then, read it several times. Its worn-out pages were soft in my hands. Familiar. Tears welled up in my eyes as the spell broke. There's no place like home.

And so, that first day and night, though I was perplexed, off-kilter, and felt like an alien who'd returned home, I didn't think once about soothing myself through writing. I didn't even ask where my copy of *I, Robot* with my writings in it was. And though sometimes the walls felt too close, and there was an occasional bump coming from my closet, and a sad howl from somewhere far away, I slept well. I slept until the next afternoon.

• • •

"Nnedi, get up," my mother said. I opened my eyes to her worried face. "You can't sleep the whole day."

I couldn't believe how long I had slept. I hadn't dreamed a thing, dwelling only in a dark abyss of slumber. But I still felt tired. How could this be? I'd been fine the day before and the day before that. I had been sleeping not great but adequately since I came home. My mother returned to my room fifteen minutes later when I still hadn't gotten up. This time she forced me out of bed by pulling the covers off me.

"Get up!" she said more firmly.

I sighed. I didn't know it at the time but I was sinking into an abyss deeper than the one I fell into while I slept. The abyss was singing me a sweet lullaby as it gently pulled me in. I was helpless against it, but my mother was not. My mother's a powerful woman. I groaned, pushing myself up. She stood beside me as I made my way to the bathroom. A plastic seat was set up in the bathtub.

I couldn't get into the tub without help and so for the millionth time, I was humiliated. It was one thing to get naked in front of the nurses; it was another to have to do it in front of my mother. The woman who gave birth to me. The woman who would probably be curious about how much her daughter's body had changed since her daughter started guarding her privacy years ago. I grumbled but succumbed. Later I'd have to endure the eyes of my sisters when my mother wasn't home to help me.

Back in the hospital, after physical therapy, my parents would often ask me to do a little more exercise with the weights, with the elastic band, with whatever. I'd usually be exhausted and reluctant. Quite a few times they forced me to do these extra exercises. They didn't understand how difficult it was. Or at least, they didn't understand on every level. I later realized that this was a good thing. Sometimes what you don't understand keeps you from seeing certain obstacles and in not seeing them, you unknowingly scale them. If they had understood, they wouldn't have pushed me so hard. And if they hadn't pushed me so hard, I wouldn't have been able to later dig my heels in and push myself. Nonetheless, on this day at home, which was about two weeks after my return, it was all just too much.

I was still too weak to use my walker regularly, so when I was upstairs I often used the wheelchair. After my bath, my mother helped me up the stairs and then I wheeled toward the kitchen. I wanted to read the day's comics from the *Chicago Sun-Times*. I needed my daily dose of *Garfield*. I wheeled into the kitchen, bumping into the doorway as I entered. I wheeled backward and forward to get through the doorway correctly. I looked on the kitchen table where the newspaper usually was. There was no newspaper. I groaned, irritated.

My mother was chopping onions and spinach leaves to put into her tomatoey stew. There were plantain slices frying in the broiler. The kitchen was warm and the moisture in the air dampened my skin. It smelled heavenly, but at the moment I didn't care. My mother glanced at me, then set her attention back on what she was doing.

This irritated me that much more. Couldn't she see that I was looking for something? Couldn't she help me or something? Why the hell did I need help searching for a simple newspaper, anyway?! I grumbled, my temper flaring and then settling. I wheeled forward, past the kitchen to the mudroom, where the recycling bin was. If the day's paper wasn't on the kitchen table, there were two places it would be. I hoped it was in the recycling bin. If it wasn't, then it was in my parents' room on their bed, where my father liked to read it. And that meant being helped up the stairs, someone lugging the wheelchair up behind me, and then a carpeted floor. Wheeling on a carpeted floor was like wheeling through molasses. My arms were strong, but everyone eventually gets tired.

I bumped hard into the doorway to the mudroom, banging my foot. I didn't feel anything, but it looked horrible. It mashed against the wall like a slab of brown rubber. I frowned, hot tears stinging my eyes. *Shit*, I thought. I didn't see any blood and this wasn't the first time I'd seen my foot mashed like this but . . . *shit*. I glanced into the red recycling bin: it was empty. I shook my head, tears flying from my eyes. I took a deep breath, but that didn't help. My mind was snapping in two. My mind was like a stick being held at each end and bent until splinters of wood started popping up. Cracking and splitting and fracturing. Breaking.

"Dammit!" I screamed. "DAMmit!"

Sobbing, I didn't turn around when I heard my mother's footsteps. Instead I bared my teeth, wheeled backward and then forward with all my might. The footrests smashed into the wall. I wheeled backward and did it again. And again. With each hit, there was another bump sound that wasn't caused by me. It was like someone was standing beside me kicking the wall with a strong leg each time I hit it with the wheelchair.

"What is your problem!" my mother yelled, stepping around me, a large spoon in her hand, red stew dripping on the floor. A limp leaf of spinach hung from the tip.

My father came striding down the hall, but I still didn't turn around.

"DAMMIT!"

Bash! Then the sound of a kick.

"DAMMIT!"

BASH! The sound of a kick.

"Goddy, I think we need to get her some psychological help," I heard my mother tell my father.

"Nnedi!" my father shouted. "Stop that! Now!"

"DAMMIT!" *Bash*. Another kick.

"Nnedi!"

"DAMMIT!" *Bash*.

The word echoed in my head, in a big circle. DAMmit dammit DAMMIT! Out of breath, I stopped, suddenly feeling unlike myself, and not liking myself. I covered my face with my hands and closed my eyes, wheezing. "Dammit," I gasped one more time.

I let my mother wheel me back to the kitchen. Behind me, the big pot of stew bubbled away. I calmed.

"Are you okay now?" my father asked me.

"I couldn't find the newspaper," I whispered.

My parents looked at each other. I quickly turned my chair around and headed back down the hall. A part of me wondered who was kicking the wall whenever I bashed my wheelchair into it. A quieter part of me knew and understood. When I reached my room, I had to wait for my parents to come and help me down the stairs.

• • •

During those early months at home I wrote things. Bits and pieces. Some of what I wrote were personal thoughts and creepy musings. Other times I wrote about the flying woman and other little stories. I'd have moments where I'd just "start to think and then I['d] sink into the paper, like I was ink," to quote Mos Def, one of my favorite rappers. The copy of *I, Robot* with my initial scribblings had to have been packed and brought home but I never saw it again. I didn't miss it, because I was always writing, and it wasn't about keeping the things I wrote as much as it was about the act of writing them.

I had strange dreams, despite the fact that I was getting enough sleep. I was so tired. Tired of the whole thing. Of course, this didn't make a difference. It didn't change anything. I could hear the wind whipping and raging and I wished I could have just walked outside. The air would have been warm and humid, heavy with droplets of water. Drinkable. If I were outside, I'd have been like a frog, drinking the air with my skin. And as it was wet outside, it was turbulent and chaotic, unpredictable, so maybe I would have been a little scared to stand in the wind.

Progress was slow, but I got better. Along with physical therapy, I began to go to the gym too. This was a different type of nightmare, because most people here were able-bodied. Never in my life had I felt so self-conscious entering a gym. However, I endured the stares that asked *What happened to her?* and did what I needed to do there. For leg exercises, I'd have to use the lightest weight and it would often take me forever just to get on the machine. It was humiliating and humbling.

I was still frail, my belly was still caved in and my legs were still thin, but they were getting stronger. And as I fell into the routine of the health club, I grew more comfortable going there. I learned later that many of the people who worked there were watching my progress with interest. They'd watched me go from the walker to the side walker to the quad cane. And they were waiting for the day I'd walk into the gym with nothing in my hands but my Walkman.

What they didn't know was that after spending about an hour exercising my body, I'd go home and exercise my mind by writing and reading, expanding over worlds and times.

Around this time, I discovered the *X-Men* animated series and was fascinated by Wolverine, his adamantium skeleton, and his rage. I had my own rage and doctors had done something to my skeleton, too. I spent most of my time downstairs because it was so difficult and scary to get up the seven steps to the main floor and I was still dealing with pain from my healing scar.

Despite all this, it was all about to turn up a notch. In a week and a half, I would leave my brooding cocoon and head back to school. I was going to return to the place I'd left a few months ago where people knew me as an athlete. The question "What happened to you?" was going to follow me like a dog.

10 My Singularity

It was my first day back at the University of Illinois, but I didn't want to get out of the car. My legs were frozen; I clutched my cane with strong hands.

Staring out at the students entering and leaving the dormitory building, I couldn't breathe. Everyone looked so normal. So sun-drenched. So relaxed. As if they'd had the best summers of their lives. A group of students I knew were sitting and talking in their usual spot outside the dorm entrance. Some of them smoked cigarettes, two played hacky sack. Just a few inches older, a few centimeters wiser. A few new faces. But all was essentially the same. Except for me.

I wasn't the same. I had a healing scar that went from the nape of my neck to my tailbone. I was at least ten pounds under the weight I'd been when I left here in May. I could no longer move easily or freely. And I had empowered spirits bouncing about my mind. As I did when I slid into the water to relearn how to walk at the hospital, I simply stopped thinking about all this and submitted to what I was. What I was was what I was. I was okay. To me. I got out of the car. Slowly.

Before I'd even reached my dorm room, I had been asked by eight people, "What happened?"

Surgery gone wrong.
Technology and science gone awry.
Medical mistake.
Victim of fate.
A relative in Nigeria worked juju on me.
Aliens.
"It's a long story," I usually answered.

Once alone in my room, when my thoughts grew too dark, interesting things sprang and sprouted from the cracks. I wrote down fragments of these things, about the tree outside my window, the smoky winding images I saw when I listened to Wu-Tang Clan, the psychedelic grasshoppers and praying mantises from my morphine hallucinations. I drew from the world around me, but also the furious part of me that still felt robbed of her superpowers.

• • •

The day I met Arnell Damani Harris I was wearing platform black Chuck Taylors and trying not to fall in front of what looked like hundreds of people. I was in line to register for a class and my middle sister, Ngozi, was with me. In the line beside us were two very tall young men. While I dealt with my classes, my sister made annoying goo-goo eyes at the taller boy, who was about six six. When the four of us got through registration, we stepped to the side and started talking.

Damani was gregarious, extroverted, and opinionated. What struck me most were two things: He had beautiful catlike eyes and at some point in the conversation he took my cane and wouldn't give the damn thing back. He'd stood there smiling at me, twirling it like a baton. He even twirled it around his back. I stood there barely hearing a word he said because I was concentrating so heavily on my cane, too shy to ask for it back. Eventually, he noticed the look on my face, laughed that laugh of his, and returned my cane.

• • •

A couple of months later Damani came to my dorm room. He was starting rehearsals for a play he was directing and rehearsals happened to be two minutes from my dorm. He'd shown up without calling, so my room was in its most natural form. There were notebooks strewn about my bed and candy bar wrappers scattered around my word processor. He looked at the mess, glanced at the clay lady on my dresser, and turned to me.

"Did you change your major yet?" he asked.

I shrugged. It was still the first semester of my second year and I was in flux. I hated my classes, especially the science ones. I'd lost faith in science. I didn't feel like listening to any of the passionate, often reverential, lectures about molecules, anatomy, the exactness of measurement, and experimentation. I loved the entomology class I was taking, but that just wasn't enough to pull me through. I felt it all boiled down to bullshit when things got real. Science had failed me. And I certainly didn't want to study it.

“Nah, I’m still premed,” I said. I shrugged. “I’m not attached to it or anything. Not anymore. But what would I change it to?”

He brought out one of the epic letters I’d written to him and I cringed. I was *always* writing to him; they were a combination of love letter, storytelling, and just my general strangeness. I never knew if he actually read them or not (a couple of decades later he told me he’d read and kept nearly every single one), but I got a kick out of the possibility. I never wanted to talk to him about them; I liked the closeness of the words and distance of the pages. In that moment, I wished he’d fold up the letter and put it back in his pocket.

“Maybe you should be a literature major,” he said, glancing at my always-expanding book collection. I was currently tinting my world with the soft magic of Alice Hoffman’s *Illumination Night*. I was enamored with Hoffman’s American-style magical realism. It was the real world as a place in which mysticism was a natural part. Hoffman presented the world similarly to the way I saw it. I’d initially picked up the book because I liked the title.

“Literature?” I said. “But what would I do with that?”

Damani shrugged. “Teach or something.”

I scowled. Stand in front of a class and talk? I didn’t like that idea.

Then Damani said one of the most valuable things anyone has ever said to me. “Or, since you’re good at writing stories,” he said, waving the letter at me, “maybe you should take a creative writing class.”

I considered asking him "What's creative writing?" but I didn't want to sound stupid, so I just said, "I'll check it out." I was so enamored with Mr. Damani Arnell Harris that the next semester I signed up for an introduction to creative writing class without really looking at the course description.

The result was immediate. That class aligned all the planets scattered about my shattered universe. As I sat there listening and learning and eventually writing, everything came into focus. It was my Big Bang. My singularity. I finally *heard* my calling.

I didn't particularly stand out in that first course, but grades and attention from professors don't determine everything. Sometimes the burn is quiet, gradual, unassuming, private. I learned what a short story was in that class. I learned that a story had a beginning, a middle, and an end. That there was voice, point of view, tense, and style. All these things I'd known from consuming novels for a decade and a half, but not on a conscious level.

In this class I wrote my first true short story, my first piece of fiction. It was called "The House of Deformities." The story was nine parts nonfiction and one part fantasy and set in Nigeria. I based the story on an incident my sisters and I had involving a strange roadside restaurant on our way to Port Harcourt International Airport. In the story, I changed my name to Adaobi, combined my sisters into one character, and tweaked one detail so I could call it fiction. I wrote the story late at night in my dorm room and the experience was distinctly different from any homework assignment I'd ever done. By this time, after all I'd been through, I'd been broken, I was open, I was ready. And the gems I'd been carrying began to tumble right out through the cracks. Here is an excerpt from "The House of Deformities" (which was published two decades later in my short story collection, *Kabu Kabu*):

> Outside was what Ngozi thought was a restaurant. People sat at wobbly tables drinking Fanta and Heineken beer and dishing up fufu with their hands and dipping it in spicy okra or egusi soup. The front of the "restaurant" was open. Adaobi wondered what they did when it rained. She could see two women cooking in a kitchen-like area at the back. She couldn't see, but she imagined that they were sweating and probably very tired.
>
> "We're stopping here for some drinks, so if you have to go to the bathroom, Ike says it's around the back," their father said. Their parents had become a lot more relaxed over the last three weeks. They were thousands of miles away from their busy lives. Ngozi was glad to see them without their pagers and having such a great time. They hadn't been back to Nigeria since before she was born, which Ngozi thought was way too long.
>
> Ngozi looked at the decrepit building with a rusting red metal gate. The air smelled of burnt marshmallows and Highlife was playing from a radio somewhere inside. Smoke billowed from the back and behind the whole building was lush forest.
>
> "Come on, Adaobi," Ngozi said, grabbing her little sister's arm. "I have to go to the bathroom and I'm not going behind there by myself."

And oh the things my sisters and I saw when we opened that gate that led to the back of that strange roadside restaurant along that southern Nigerian road. My sisters and I had been eight, nine, and ten years old when we encountered the pink ducklings, the baby bulldog puppies, the wizened old woman with a cleaver, the table full of meat she was chopping up, and the meat-stealing vultures. And we'd coined this place "the House of Deformities." When I was asked to make up my own story in that class, my mind flew right to that strange restaurant.

Writing the story was a spark to dry kindling. The act of creating a story had a delicious sensation and I instantly fell madly in love with it. It felt like stepping off the edge of a cliff on purpose when you subconsciously knew you had the ability to fly. It took me to a place where I didn't need to walk. And it came so damn easily. What was most breathtaking was that even before I submitted it to the professor, I knew it was good. *I* knew. And I didn't need anyone to validate this knowledge.

I don't recall the grade I received on that first short story. I don't recall the response of the class when the story was critiqued, except that it wasn't greatly disliked. None of that mattered to me. What mattered was how I felt when I read my own stories. It felt goooood. And so I wrote some more. I started writing stories for myself, between, above, below, and on top of school assignments. By the time the semester was over, I'd stopped using my cane and I was writing my first novel.

• • •

It was summer again, a year after my surgery. I was walking without a cane. I was strong, but I would never be the same. My proprioception was what had mainly suffered. The sense of touch in the bottom half of my legs and my feet had vastly decreased and the soles of my feet, which used to be so ticklish, no longer were. My feet now felt perpetually asleep. If I was not looking at my legs, there were times when it would feel as if they'd disappeared and I'd have to rely on my body's natural instincts to keep from falling over. And though my legs were strong, if I walked too fast, I lost the ability to walk in a straight line.

Despite all this, I was happy. I'd tumbled into the abyss and worked my way out. I'd been suddenly paralyzed and now I could walk again. I'd changed my major from premed to rhetoric (at the University of Illinois, U-C, this was "creative writing"), and I was writing more than ever. I was also testing out journalism by interning at a local newspaper called *The Star*. Writing fiction was most natural to me, but there was a joy I felt in writing feature stories and seeing them published as well.

One day my editor gave me a big assignment. I don't remember exactly what the story was about but it involved a family and it was important to the newspaper. There was one problem—a problem that only those who knew me well would have recognized. I was set to interview the family at 7 p.m. At night. But I couldn't drive at night.

I'd tried doing it once, some months after I'd returned home and was still walking with a cane. Once I could walk, driving wasn't an issue. But at night, things got weird. In the dark, I couldn't see my legs and had to rely on proprioception. People do this all the time without a thought. That's normal. However, I was no longer normal and I should have been more conscious of this in the case of driving. One night while driving home on an empty road from somewhere, I came to an intersection. When I tried to brake, I couldn't feel where the brake was. Suddenly, it was as if my legs had disappeared, right there in the car, behind the wheel of a two-ton vehicle going forty miles per hour.

The more I panicked, the less I could feel. I'd gone right through the intersection before I was finally able to find the brake with my foot. Thankfully, the intersection was empty. I was lucky. From that point on, I stopped driving at night.

Nevertheless, I really, really wanted to do this story, so I decided to try something. That afternoon I rushed to Walgreens and bought a simple black Eveready flashlight and a pack of four D batteries, two for the flashlight and two for backup. The place where I was to do the interview was forty-five minutes away. I was so hell-bent on doing the story that I barreled forth.

I didn't tell my parents, sisters, or anyone how terrified I was about driving at night with the flashlight. I just did it. I got dressed, got directions, got in the car with my flashlight, flicked it on, and started the car. I didn't sit in the car for even a minute worrying about what could happen, how hard it would be, or how I'd use the flashlight. I just went. As I drove I intuitively knew when to grab the flashlight, flick it on, check my feet, nod with assurance, click it off, and put it back in my lap. The sight of my feet near the pedals assured my brain that my feet and legs were where they needed to be. It was just that natural, just that smooth. And just like that, I hurdled the issue of night driving and arrived in time to interview the family.

To this day this is how I drive at night. I keep the flashlight right in the center console between the front seats so I can reach it even when I'm driving as the sun goes down. I hold it in my right hand. The flashlight seems to become a part of my being, an augmentation. It's yet another way that I have become something new, something more.

My fused spine limits how much I can rotate so don't expect me to turn around if you call me from behind. I can't look up at the stars without holding on to something. I can walk far, but I have to do it slowly. I will never be able to do a backbend again. Well, not until the year 2029, at least.

11 Machine

Sticks and stones and silicone.
Metal limbs, artificial bones.
Legs like pins, lacking muscle tone.
All things sturdy. All things man-grown.

I wrote these words while still in the throes of the Breaking, gazing at the cover of *I, Robot*. As my body settled into its cyborg self, the writer in me, now aware of herself, also grew into a new clear voice, a voice that had always been there somewhere. Themes of hybrid humans became my own. I rooted stories in contrasts, stories like this:

> I stood in a place where all things were safe. When I looked down, I had legs of steel. They were shiny and cold. I, Robot. I am a robot and I have not gone mad yet. I have no intension of killing my creator, though I have good reason. He made me this way.
>
> However, at the moment, his orders make sense. And sense is what I live by. Keep my metal joints and gadgets well oiled and maintained and I will always protect my own existence. It's

the fighter in me. But I hate being a robot. I am competitive, yet in this body, I can't always do what I want to do. I'd have created something far more complex if I were my creator.

I'd have made me more fluid in motion and soft in texture and material. I'd have stretched my arms and legs nine feet in length, shortened my midsection some more. I'd have been like a four-limbed spider, but soft . . . and unbreakable, yielding. Now I'm just confused, so I roll my thoughts in my mind. Around and around. He must think I've gone mad, but I haven't. My activity interests him, so he brings his colleagues to study me. I continue pacing.

In circles. It keeps my body working and functioning, but I am getting nowhere. As I walk in circles that become smaller and smaller, I begin to think, maybe he's lying. Maybe he didn't create me. And if he didn't create me then who did and if he didn't create me why shouldn't I kill him? For if he is not my creator, then he is my enslaver. As the circle shrinks, I can only come to one conclusion . . .

It was over a decade before I actually read *I, Robot*, and it wasn't the beaten-up copy James had given me in the hospital. That copy, lost to the ages, had served a much higher purpose. Within its pages was a unique discovery. Written on the inside flap, in my long narrow handwriting, around the printed words of Isaac Asimov, in pen because I didn't like writing in pencil. My hand scribbled words and I disregarded the printed words to write my own stories.

A door had opened with those scribblings. And I stepped through. The words I wrote in the margins of that book led me months later to write my first official short story in a creative writing class. Writing that short story led me to write novels, the second of which is based on the flying woman who sprang from my scribblings in that copy of *I, Robot*. It begins like this:

> It was April. 1925. Eighty degrees with a nice breeze. She was twenty years old. Hovering above in the dark, she looked down at her village with disgust. But she didn't fly off just yet.

With these few lines, I was off. The day I wrote them, bedridden, broken, and squeezed by pain in that hospital, the wind was howling outside. Wind strong enough to catch and then take a woman who could fly wherever she wanted to go. I wasn't diminished by my limitations. I've become more, greater. Before the Breaking, the day I awoke paralyzed from the waist down, I could not have written these words, this world, this character. The cracks the storyteller in me required weren't there. It was because of and after the Breaking and my subsequent journey that I acquired this part of my self.

Yet the Breaking by itself, it turned out, wasn't quite enough. My paralysis and recovery led me to writing, but it would take an additional journey, a journey through my ancestral home of Nigeria, for me to meet and bond with an African-rooted form of science fiction.

The flying woman, the character whom I eventually named Arro-yo, ultimately left our world of the past and flew right into a future where advanced biotechnology had been woven into a Nigerian way of life. However, I wrote that part later, after I'd returned to Nigeria. In many ways, the synthesis I experienced when I returned to my father's village of Arondizuogu mirrored the one my more recently created character Binti experienced. I spoke of her in my 2017 TED Talk, "Sci-fi stories that imagine a future Africa":

> In a distant-future part of Africa, Binti is a mathematical genius of the Himba ethnic group. She's been accepted into a university on another planet and she decides to go. Carrying the blood of her people in her veins. Adorned with the teachings, ways, even the land, Binti leaves Earth. As the story progresses, she becomes not other, but more.
>
> Binti could never have become the great heroine she becomes if she didn't break her relationship with her family by sneaking away from home to attend a university on another galaxy. She loved her family and she loves her culture, but she also knew she wanted more and the only way to obtain it was to leave in a way she knew would devastate those she loved dearly.
>
> By embarking on this incredible journey, Binti is changed forever, on both a mental and a physical level. She is altered all the way down to her very DNA, which becomes blended with alien DNA. By the end of the series, she is far more than she

would ever have been if she had stayed home. For better and for worse. But mostly for better.

Like my space-faring character Binti, I had to leave what was normal to become greater still. It was in these strange, deep, old, and new waters that I was free. And also like Binti, after venturing into, being broken by, and changed by the unknown, it was the return home that brought it all together.

My parents started taking my siblings and me back to Nigeria when we were all very young. My first time was when I was seven. To my imaginative eyes, Nigeria was paradise. On that first trip, I remember my grandmother putting a bowl of fried plantain in front of me. I love fried plantain and it was more plantain than I'd ever seen in my life, good plantain being difficult to find in the United States back then. I went a little mad. I started stuffing my face as though someone was going to take that bowl away from me. I ate so much so fast that I ended up throwing it all up.

My cousins and I were thick as thieves, especially me and my cousin and age-mate Adaobi. I chased and befriended chickens, caught and documented a plethora of exotic insects. I tried to learn Igbo and the terrible American accent I spoke it with was laughed at so much that I eventually gave up. And oh the strange incidents and adventures.

Still, as I grew older, and after my experience with paralysis opened my mind wider, I began to observe and understand more. Those trips were stressful, especially for my parents, who had so many relatives to please, being the Ones Who Made It to America, Land of Milk and Honey. All six of the additional giant suitcases we brought were filled with things for, well, everyone. The roads weren't just fun to drive on, they were damn dangerous. Those weren't family friends accompanying us on the way to the village, those were AK-47–armed guards.

And then there were the girls I saw coming back from the stream that day in Arondizuogu when I was in my twenties. They were carrying large containers of water on their heads, water that they would pour into larger plastic barrels to be used for the day. The water sloshed a bit on their heads and they held their cell phones away so they wouldn't get wet. From that moment, I started looking out for technology in Nigeria. The only TV channels we received in the village were BET and MTV, and this gave a lot of people some questionable ideas about African Americans. I noticed early on that mobile tech was popular and incorporated into society faster in Nigeria than in the United States, in part because of unreliable infrastructure (a desktop computer had a better future in the United States than in Nigeria where electrical power was far less reliable).

I wasn't seeing *this* Africa in narratives and this frustrated me. The Africa I was seeing in literature was a place of the past that was left behind, a place whose value was in it being "the cradle of civilization" millennia ago, a place whose culture many liked to appreciate as a place they'd left behind and then from a distance, a place that had no specifics (people went to "Africa," not a country or particular city in Africa), a place whose greatness existed only in its imagined state where colonization didn't happen. The part of Africa that *I* knew existed and that was very much in the present and hurtling into the future in a really cool, unique way—I wanted to write about *that* place.

The struggle that I sublimate through all my writing has been in my actively, willingly facing, breaking, and fusing my American and Nigerian cultures into what many of us call "Naijamerican" ("Naija" is Nigerian slang for "Nigerian" or "Nigeria"). And it has been in my learning to live with and embrace my strange crippled body.

Most traditional science fiction depicts a white world where I was not able to freely exist. But in the science fiction of what I've come to call "Africanfuturism" (which is somewhat similar to Afrofuturism, but is specifically and more directly rooted in African culture, history, mythology, and perspective, where the center is non-Western), my characters inhabit worlds in which I can fight, play, invent, run, leap, and fly.

As I continue to evolve and grow, so do my dreams and speculations. In a short story that appears in *Twelve Tomorrows* (an anthology published by *MIT Technology Review*) called "Heart of the Matter," I speculate about a Nigerian president who enters office knowing he has a heart condition caused by years of severe diabetes.

During his term, his condition worsens and he has to undergo a special heart transplant, one that gifts him with a 3D-printed heart made from the harvested healthy cells of his own heart and fortified with spinach leaves. He becomes the world's first "xyborg" president (xylem are plant veins). The new heart strengthens his body and significantly lengthens his life. However, there is trouble because the people begin to question whether he's even a human being anymore, let alone the same man they elected. Those worries and people taking advantage of those worries lead to an attempted coup.

In my short comic in Marvel's *Venomverse: War Stories* anthology titled "Blessing in Disguise" and the subsequent one-shot issue *Under the Bridge* (featured in the Black Panther series *Long Live the King*), I wrote about a Nigerian girl named Ngozi whose legs were destroyed a year earlier in a car accident. Ngozi joins forces with an alien symbiotic organism to become a shape-shifting superhero that not only can walk but also fly, and much more. The strong will she uses to control the symbiote is one she developed while learning to live in a world in which she was disabled.

Nigeria was my door to science fiction. The opening of this door restored my faith in science after science failed me. And once I was back as a proud disciple, I was free to embrace my own cyborgity. Something just had to break first.

"I move about the world in my own way."

—Nnedi Okorafor

12 The Beach

The sand beneath my feet shifts with each step and the surface is uneven. At the same time, the friction of the sand on the soles of my feet gives my brain more information, improving my proprioception. My robotic gait toward the water is meandering but strong. And if I fall, the surface wouldn't be that hard.

I focus on the rushing and retreating waves up ahead and the fresh briny smell of the ocean air. I'm aware of my exposed back but I don't feel the usual self-conscious sting because the beach is empty. Only the crabs peeking from their holes, grasshoppers hiding in the beach grass, and passing butterflies and sea birds can see my oddly curved back. And sometimes my ancestors.

I put a foot in the retreating water and, if I concentrate quite hard, I can relish the sucking sensation of the sand beneath my foot. The ocean washes over my feet and I move farther in. I begin to wobble but I push forward. Before I fall, I throw myself in the water. And then I'm flying.

ACKNOWLEDGMENTS

I've been writing this book since 1994, starting it months after losing and regaining my ability to walk. I needed to remember exactly how I felt at that time, in the thick of it. The first forty pages I wrote were the greatest number of pages I'd ever written at the time, and my word processor erased it all when it suffered a mysterious glitch. I started rewriting the pages that very same day. Over the years, I overwrote this book (it used to be four times longer). I chopped it down. I put it aside. I came back to it. I always knew I would complete it.

My first thank-yous go to my ancestors for seeing and pushing me through all this, being at my back, my sides, and in my front. I would like to thank my parents, Dr. Godwin Okorafor and Dr. Helen Okorafor, and my siblings Ifeoma, Ngozi and Emezie, for being my foundation for everything. Thanks to my daughter Anyaugo, who heard me reading this book aloud while I was editing it and came into the room to listen. Thanks to my nephews and niece Dika, Obi, Chinedu. And many thanks to my TED Books editor Michelle Quint for her patience and keen eye.

ABOUT THE AUTHOR

Nnedi Okorafor is a Nigerian-American author of African-based science fiction, fantasy, and magical realism for children and adults. Her works include *Who Fears Death* (currently being developed by HBO into a TV series), the Binti novella trilogy (currently being developed by Hulu into a TV series), the *Book of Phoenix*, the *Akata* books, and *Lagoon*. She is the winner of Hugo, Nebula, World Fantasy, Locus, and Lodestar awards, and her debut novel *Zahrah the Windseeker* won the prestigious Wole Soyinka Prize for Literature. Nnedi has also written comics for Marvel, including *Black Panther: Long Live the King* and *Wakanda Forever*, featuring the Dora Milaje and Shuri characters. She is also the writer of the science fiction comic series published by Dark Horse called *LaGuardia*. She lives with her daughter Anyaugo and family in Illinois. Follow Nnedi on Twitter (as @Nnedi), Facebook, and Instagram. Learn more about Nnedi at Nnedi.com.

WATCH NNEDI OKORAFOR'S TED TALK

Nnedi Okorafor's TED Talk, available for free at TED.com, is the companion to *Broken Places & Outer Spaces: Finding Creativity in the Unexpected.*

PHOTO: RYAN LASH/TED

RELATED TALKS

Anne Lamott
12 truths I learned from life and writing
A few days before she turned 61, writer Anne Lamott decided to write down everything she knew for sure. She dives into the nuances of being a human who lives in a confusing, beautiful, emotional world, offering her characteristic life-affirming wisdom and humor on family, writing, the meaning of God, death and more.

Dayo Ogunyemi
Visions of Africa's future, from African filmmakers
By expanding boundaries, exploring possibilities, and conveying truth, films have helped change Africa's reality (even before *Black Panther*). Dayo Ogunyemi invites us to imagine Africa's future through the lens of inspiring filmmakers from across the continent, showing us how they can inspire Africa to make a hundred-year leap.

Aimee Mullins
My 12 pairs of legs
Athlete, actor, and activist Aimee Mullins talks about her prosthetic legs—she's got a dozen amazing pairs—and the superpowers they grant her: speed, beauty, an extra 6 inches of height. ... Quite simply, she redefines what the body can be.

Hugh Herr
How we'll become cyborgs and extend human potential
Humans will soon have new bodies that forever blur the line between the natural and synthetic worlds, says bionics designer Hugh Herr. In an unforgettable talk, he details "NeuroEmbodied Design," a methodology for creating cyborg function that he's developing at MIT, and shows us a future where we've augmented our bodies in a way that will redefine human potential—and, maybe, turn us into superheroes. "During the twilight years of this century, I believe humans will be unrecognizable in morphology and dynamics from what we are today," Herr says. "Humanity will take flight and soar."

MORE FROM TED BOOKS

The Hot Young Widows Club: Lessons on Survival from the Front Lines of Grief
by Nora McInerny

Whether you lost your spouse or lost your job, navigating grief is often a lonely business. Welcome to The Hot Young Widows Club. Drawing from her own life experience, Nora McInerny offers a wise, humorous roadmap and caring community for anyone going through a challenging life moment.

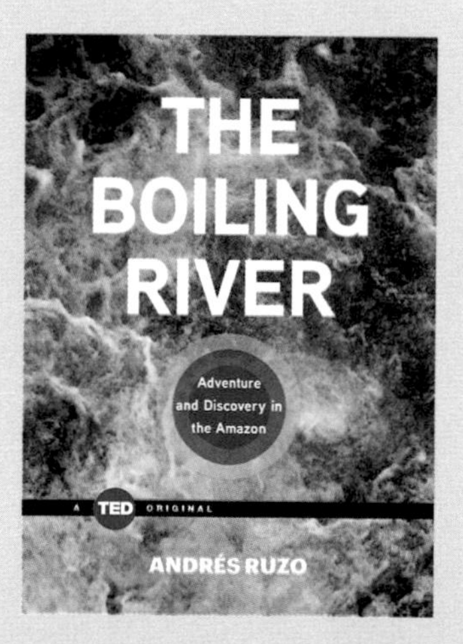

The Boiling River: Adventure and Discovery in the Amazon
by Andrés Ruzo

In this exciting adventure mixed with amazing scientific discovery, a young, exuberant explorer and geoscientist journeys deep into the Amazon—where rivers boil and legends come to life.